Pebble® Plus

Physical Science

Gravity All Around

by David Conrad

CAPSTONE PRESS
a capstone imprint

Pebble Plus is published by Capstone Press,
1710 Roe Crest Drive, North Mankato, Minnesota 56003.
www.capstonepub.com

 Books published by Capstone Press are manufactured with paper
containing at least 10 percent post-consumer waste.

Library of Congress Cataloging-in-Publication Data
Conrad, David (David J.), 1967–
  Gravity all around / by David Conrad
      p. cm.—(Pebble Plus. Physical science)
  Includes index.
  ISBN 978-1-4296-6606-0 (library binding)
  1. Gravity—Juvenile literature. 2. Gravitation—Juvenile literature.
  I. Title.
  QC178.C6374 2011
  531'.14—dc22   2010034310

Summary: Simple text and color photographs introduce gravity, including its history and how it affects Earth.

Editorial Credits

Gillia Olson, editor; Veronica Correia, designer; Eric Gohl, media researcher; Laura Manthe, production specialist

Photo Credits

The Bridgeman Art Library International/©Look and Learn/Private Collection/James Edwin McConnell, 13; The Royal
      Institution, London, UK/Robert Hannah, 15
Capstone Studio/Karon Dubke, cover, 9, 20–21 (all)
iStockphoto/posteriori, 5
Shutterstock/Andresr, 19 (boy on right); Blackbirds, 19 (background); Jacek Chabraszewski, 7; Mandy Godbehear, 1;
      Panos Karapanagiotis, 11; Ronald van der Beek, 17; Thomas M Perkins, 19 (boy on left)

Note to Parents and Teachers

The Physical Science series supports national standards related to physical science. This
book describes and illustrates gravity. The images support early readers in understanding the
text. The repetition of words and phrases helps early readers learn new words. This book
also introduces early readers to subject-specific vocabulary words, which are defined in the
Glossary section. Early readers may need assistance to read some words and to use the Table of
Contents, Glossary, Read More, Internet Sites, and Index sections of the book.

Printed in the United States of America in North Mankato, Minnesota.
052013
007382R

Table of Contents

What Is Gravity?

It makes a dropped glass

fall to the floor.

It keeps bouncing balls

from flying off into space.

It's a force called gravity.

Gravity can't be seen,

but it's all around you.

When you jump,

gravity pulls you

back to the ground.

To see how gravity works, whirl a ball on a string. The string is like gravity. It keeps the ball from flying away. If the string breaks, the ball flies off.

Proving Gravity

In the 300s BC, Aristotle of ancient Greece thought about why objects fell to the ground. He thought heavy things fell faster than light things.

People believed Aristotle until the early 1600s. Then, Italian scientist Galileo studied gravity. He proved that all objects fall at the same speed.

In 1665 Sir Isaac Newton proved that gravity pulls all objects toward each other. He discovered that the moon circles Earth because of gravity.

More or Less Gravity

If Earth had less gravity,

it would be like the moon.

Earth would have no water,

air, plants, or animals.

They would all float away.

If Earth had more gravity, we
would be as flat as pancakes
on the ground. Imagine how
different life would be if Earth
had more or less gravity!

Stronger than Gravity

What You Need

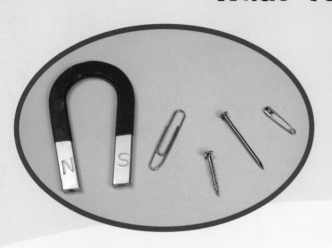

- 1 safety pin
- 1 magnet
- other small metal objects

1 Drop a safety pin.
Gravity makes it fall.

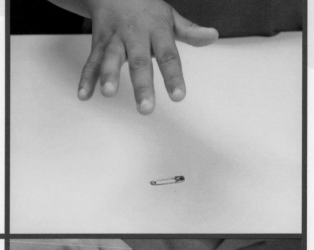

2 Hold the safety pin next
to a magnet. Then let it go.
Try the other metal objects too.
What happens?

3 The metal objects stick to the magnet! The magnet is stronger than gravity.

Glossary

ancient—belonging to a time long ago

discover—to find out about something

force—a power that causes something to change or move

gravity—the force that pulls all things to one another

speed—how fast or slow something moves

whirl—to turn in a circle

Read More

Manolis, Kay. *Gravity.* Blastoff! Readers: First Science. Minneapolis: Bellwether Media, 2009.

Mason Crest Publishers. *Why Why Why Do Astronauts Float in Space?* Broomall, Penn.: Mason Crest Publishers, 2009.

Murray, Julie. *Gravity.* A Buddy Book. First Science. Edina, Minn.: ABDO Pub., 2007.

Internet Sites

FactHound offers a safe, fun way to find Internet sites related to this book. All of the sites on FactHound have been researched by our staff.

Here's all you do:

Visit *www.facthound.com*

Type in this code: 9781429666060

Super-cool stuff! Check out projects, games and lots more at www.capstonekids.com

Index

Word Count: 198
Grade: 1
Early-Intervention Level: 23